GOONA GOONA

Megan Terry

*Music by
Lynn Herrick
Structured by
Jo Ann Schmidman*

BROADWAY PLAY PUBLISHING INC
New York
www.broadwayplaypublishing.com
info@broadwayplaypublishing.com

GOONA GOONA
© Copyright 1991 Megan Terry
© Copyright 1991 music by the Omaha Magic Theater

All rights reserved. This work is fully protected under the copyright laws of the United States of America. No part of this publication may be photocopied, reproduced, stored in a retrieval system, or transmitted, in any form or by any means, electronic, mechanical, recording, or otherwise, without the prior permission of the publisher. Additional copies of this play are available from the publisher.

Written permission is required for live performance of any sort. This includes readings, cuttings, scenes, and excerpts. For amateur and stock performances, please contact Broadway Play Publishing Inc. For all other rights please contact The Marton Agency Inc, 1 Union Sq W, #815, NY NY 10003, 212 255-1908.

Cover photo by Megan Terry

First edition: November 1991
This edition: October 2017
I S B N: 978-0-88145-101-6

Book design: Marie Donovan
Word processing: WordMarc Composer Plus
Typographic controls: Xerox Ventura Publisher 2.0 PE
Typeface: Palatino

ORIGINAL PRODUCTION

GOONA GOONA was first performed by the Omaha Magic Theater on 9 Nov 1979. The cast and creative contributors were as follows:

TEENAGER .... Jo Ann Schmidman
BEATEN MAN .... Tim Thompson
NURSE .... Gracie Lee
DR GRANVILLE GOON .... Jo Ann Schmidman
JUNE GOON .... Dyan Tison
MRS MARRIOT .... Abigail Leah
MR MARRIOT .... Wes Clowers or James Larson
GAGA GOON .... Lynn Herrick
GARFIELD GOON .... Craig McCurry
NEW NURSE .... Rob Kenney
HEAD NURSE .... Eve Felder
GOGO GOON .... Jo Ann Schmidman
GRANDMA GOON .... Jo Ann Schmidman
POLICE .... Wes Clowers or James Larson

Understudies ...... Gwen Andrews and Greg Gibson

Piano .... Dyan Tison
Guitar .... Gracie Lee
Bass .... Lynn Herrick

Musical variations and earthquake theme .... Dyan Tison
Stage manager .... Abigail Leah
Costume and set design .... Megan Terry
Costume and set execution .... Elizabeth Scheuerlein
Prop design and execution .... Elizabeth Scheuerlein
Set construction .... Craig McCurry

Original Production

Lighting design .... Colbert McClellan
Lighting technician .... Tim Thompson
Publicity .... Rose Marie Whiteley
Graphics .... Wes Clowers and Greg Gibson

CHARACTERS

DR GRANVILLE GOON, *Dad, is head of household; a successful orthopedic surgeon who considers himself a poet.*

JUNE GOON, *Mother; a homemaker; takes drugs her husband prescribes for her; abused and bewildered by her husband, when the situation gets too emotional, she goes to sleep.*

GAGA GOON, *a very bright 9-year-old girl.*

GARFIELD GOON, *a bewildered 8-year-old boy.*

GOGO GOON, *an extremely bright hyperactive 7-year-old, bordering on the demonic. She/he will carry on the cycle of abuse.*

GRANDMA GOON, GRANVILLE's *mother, who sees the role of the parent as one who shows love through punishment.*

LORNA GOON, *the dog, often kicked.*

MR and MRS MARRIOT, *the* GOONs' *next-door neighbors; good citizens, good community members who think they hear screams.*

THE KID, GRANVILLE GOON *as a young teen.*

Three VISITING NURSES, *may be played by men or women.*

POLICE, *an affable person, involved with his/her community.*

Characters

THE SINK, *one of the actors who plays a* VISITING NURSE *transforms into the sink and assists* GRANDMA *in her abuse of the Goon children.*

NOTE: DR GOON, GRANDMA, GOGO, *and* THE KID *can be played by the same actor, who may be male or female. The cycle of abuse is shown implicitly if the same actor plays all these roles, as we did in the OMT production.*

INTRODUCTION

We are surrounded by violence—violence on television, violent music. The media are full of models of violence against person and property. Psychologically, one can be violated. Much of it is insidious and hidden; a lot is out in the open, but still not acknowledged.

GOONA GOONA speaks to this violence. It is a piece about domestic violence, violence in the home, involving those we are closest to — spouses and children. We will enter the home and lives of the GRANVILLE and JUNE GOON family, an upper middle-class couple who love each other. The GOONS are a nuclear family—Dad works, Mom stays home, and they have 2.5 children—GAGA who is the eldest, GARFIELD, and GOGO, who is hyperactive and, because she may hurt herself or others, is always chained either to her bed or the cat-tree in the living room. GRANDMA GOON has physically and psychologically abused GRANVILLE, and in her mind this has paid off because he's now a successful doctor. She sees no reason not to treat her grandchildren, whom she babysits, the same. Domestic violence is learned behavior—GRANDMA taught it by example; GRANVILLE and the children will do the same.
The GOONS, if you were to ask a casual observer, are the perfect, successful, loving nuclear family.

NOTE: This play may be produced simply à la creative dramatics or Story Theatre techniques. Or, it

Introduction

may be totally produced, with full production values. Suggestions follow:

THE CHARACTERS: In the OMT production, adult actors played the child characters.

THE SET: The floor is made up of tumbling mats—rubber or any other surface suitable for tumbling and pratfalls. At the OMT, we made a soft-sculpture backdrop, which when on tour hangs on a 1" steel collapsible pipe frame measuring 10' x 20'. The backdrop is the GOON family living room—there is a large window in the high cathedral ceiling center—through it the MARRIOTS are seen and can observe the GOONS. The cat-tree, a giant soft-sculpture 2-legged scratching post (5' x 4' x 6'), is centered against the backdrop. Downstage center is a practical soft-sculpture teeter-tooter which serves as the family couch. A soft-sculpture puppet frame (4' x 6') is used to frame and highlight certain scenes.

THE COSTUMES: The costumes for the GOON family are constructed from hospital greens designed into a fashionable leisure suit for Dad, play clothes for the CHILDREN, and dresses for JUNE and GRANDMA. The GOONS wear headdresses that are like padded football helmets with yarn hair and large soft-sculpture ears sticking out. These protect the heads and offer hair and ears for abusive grabbing and twisting with no injury to the actors. GRANDMA's headdress sports a flowered hat and earrings. GOGO has premature grey hair, DR GOON has a soft-sculpture mirror coming out of his forehead, GAGA has a bow in her hair, etc.

The VISITING NURSES are informally uniformed; they are a helping team. At the OMT the nurses wore simple blue and white shirt/slack/skirt combinations.

The MARRIOTS are seen in their pajamas—she in a pretty nightgown and he in two-piece silk p.j.'s. As the POLICE, MR MARRIOT dons a uniform jacket and hat or helmet.

The GOON costumes are padded with foam rubber to accentuate character—JUNE is padded in her behind and hips, DR GOON to appear barrel-chested and broad-shouldered. GARFIELD has a big padded belly, GAGA a jester's hump, and GRANDMA has big bosoms. (GOGO is unpadded.)

MUSIC NOTE: The "Happier Than You" songs are to be sung in a mean, sour, and aggressive style.

PLAY STRUCTURE: The play structure of GOONA GOONA is that of a presentational larger-than-life Punch and Judy puppet show. Remember, when the baby cried, Punch would throw it down the steps. Slapstick and tumbling are used throughout. This directorial choice—though it may seem an exaggeration—is minimal compared to the living nightmare and enormous devastation existing within the reality of a violent household. You may find it necessary to write a program note calling your audience's attention to this reality. OMT found on our extensive tours of this play that many communities are still in states of denial about family violence.

ACT ONE

(The play opens with the KID [GRANVILLE as a child] beating up an innocent bystander with a soft-sculpture bat. These two figures can be seen in a single shaft of light. Rhythmic blows elicit percussive moans from the person being beaten. Music begins and Company enters.)

(GAGA and GARFIELD, on either side of teeter-totter, running in place, hands flopping like puppets. The KID hits them alternately with the music. With the sound of each blow, the company works out freezes—image of Defend or Protect. VISITING NURSES rush from one victim to another in an attempt to help; they too work on Protect and Defend images. An "(x)" signifies blows to an actor's padded body part.)

KID: *(Chants while piano vamps chords of song)*
After that last lightning storm
My dad blamed me—*(x)*
He was so sore, he *(x)* hit me with a tree
It made me so mad, *(x) (x)* I went hunting
Some weaker heads *(x)* to get even.

Then out of the corner of my bloodshot eye *(x)*
I saw a van load of angels
trucking on by.

Those Visiting Nurses, flying in their V—
They yelled: "Stop all that gore. *(x)*
You, teenager! Stop knocking people down
With that two-by-four." *(x)*

(x) A woman on her knees, her dress all muddy,
Was pickin' up her teeth and
Puttin' 'em in a tin.
(x) An old man, his head already bloody,
Let out a terrible roar—*(x)*
As I jumped and hit 'em
Both again with my two-by-four. *(x)*

(VISITING NURSES *cross to* KID; *try to reason with him.*)

KID: Concentratin' hard to keep the fright from
   their voice
They said, "Drop the board, kid,
There must be another choice.
We see you're angry, we see you are sore, but is
This the right way to even a score?"

(VISITING NURSES *do Protect Isolations.*)

KID: I hit and said, *(x)* "I'm not mad. *(x)* I'm not mad.
I'm glad. I'm glad and more. *(x)*
Did you ever see one kid *(x)*
Deck so many with a two-by-four?"

(VISITING NURSES *exit upstage.*)

KID: I'm not insane. *(x)* I'm not insane. *(x)*
I'm not insane. *(x)* I'm not insane. *(x)*
I'm just the guy to take the place of old John Wayne.

(VISITING NURSES *return with* DR GOON's *white coat.*)

KID: Right then the sky opened up with a pelting rain
That helped them invoke
The ghost of old John Wayne.

(VISITING NURSES *take his bat and coax the* KID *into white coat, and comfort him.*)

KID: Then they kidded me, the Kid,
Into being gentle and tame. So—
We bandaged up the bruised
And drove home the lame.

ACT ONE

(VISITING NURSES walk KID around to teeter-totter, sit him down, and exit.)

KID: They dropped me off at the institute
To find my sanity again.

(A tired JUNE enters with toy box; a soft-sculpture bat sticks out.)

JUNE: Thank God the children are in bed.

DR GOON: Thank me, you mean.

JUNE: *(Turns quickly; the bat sticking out of toy box knocks DR GOON down.)* What?

DR GOON: I said thank me.

JUNE: I'm so exhausted *(Sets box down, sits on teeter-totter)* my ears went to sleep.

DR GOON: *(In JUNE's face)* Rise and shine. Get this stuff unpacked. *(Points at toy box and around room)*

JUNE: I'm so tired I can't lift my arm.

DR GOON: This is the house you wanted. Move in!

JUNE: This is the house you wanted.

DR GOON: You wanted.

JUNE: *(Stands)* I didn't sign the papers.

DR GOON: Because you were too *tired* to lift your arm.

JUNE: I think it's strange the house is in *your* name.

DR GOON: *(Pulls soft-sculpture toys out of toy box and throws them at JUNE)* I think it's strange you don't want to unpack and decorate this new house I killed myself to buy for you.

JUNE: Wait a minute.

DR GOON: I'm tired of waiting.

JUNE: *(Catches an object, throws it back at him)* Who sent you through medical school?

DR GOON: My mother.

JUNE: You've got to be tired, too.

DR GOON: *(Dreamily)* Without my mother's vision and ambition, *(Side-flips over his shoulder to the floor)* I would have quit long ago.

JUNE: *(Starts to get up)* I paid your bills.

DR GOON: *(As* JUNE *gets to her knees,* DR GOON *grabs her by the hair and harshly whispers in her ear)* Why are you always talking about money? No wonder our kids are confused about values. *(Slaps* JUNE *on each word)* Money, money, money, money. *(Forcefully pushes* JUNE *by the back of her neck around the entire room.)* You should be thrilled to death. Look around you. Here's what money can buy.

JUNE: *(As she's being forced)* If I hadn't worked as a cocktail waitress and bellydancer we wouldn't be here right now.

DR GOON: *(Lets go of* JUNE *abruptly)* That was in another life. *(Shakes finger at her)* Don't raise your voice. *(Backhands* JUNE*)* Don't wake the kids. I don't want to have to give them a sedative.

JUNE: *(Ducks in a gesture of self-protection; angry but soft voice)* If I hadn't wiggled my fanny night after night in that phony Greek restaurant, you wouldn't be using a sterling silver scalpel today.

(The next five lines are said in a direct deadpan.)

DR GOON: Do you want a lobotomy?

JUNE: Excuse me?

DR GOON: Do you want me to remove that memory?

JUNE: You're crazy.

ACT ONE

DR GOON: I can remove that attitude, too.

(VISITING NURSES *bring on puppet frame.* JUNE *and* DR GOON *go behind puppet frame. They become highly animated, their voices change to high-pitched, quick-tempo puppet voices as in a Punch and Judy show.*)

JUNE: Just a minute. *(Spins around)* What's going on?

(DR GOON *abuses* JUNE *in a variety of ways throughout the following speech: strangles, grabs her by ears, backhands her.*)

DR GOON: That's what I'd like to know. I haven't slept in days. All you do is complain about your arm and the fact that you once worked. I don't want the kids to know what you did. Forget it! Forget it! It isn't cute anymore. And don't ever mention it at hospital staff parties. *(Mocking)* I want to know if you've started your correspondence course?

JUNE: *(Jumps on* DR GOON's *back)* I have my M.A. and I'm half-way to my Ph.D.! And I'm going to get it! I have brains, too, you know. Those kids didn't get genius IQs from you alone.

DR GOON: Of course you're going to get your degree. You have to pay for the gas your Cadillac guzzles.

JUNE: Your Lincoln needs gas, too.

DR GOON: I get eight miles to the gallon, and I can write it off.

JUNE: *(Chokes* DR GOON *while still on his back)* Big deal. You're a big deal. I'd really like to fight with you *(Collapses onto back)* but I'm too tired. *(Pops up)* I'm going to get my psychiatric-social worker license and then I can write you and my car off too!

DR GOON: *(Throws* JUNE *off his back)* Not your car, you dope. Your gas. But in your job you can't drive a Cadillac. *Your* patients would freak with envy.

JUNE: *(Comes up on knees, face just peeking over bottom of puppet frame, cowering)* What about your *patients*?

DR GOON: I need a Lincoln for my patients. They wouldn't trust me if I drove a compact.

JUNE: I suppose you'd like to see me on a moped? *(Gestures as if on moped)*

DR GOON: It has a certain charm, but your *(DR GOON turns JUNE around so that her large, padded behind is in the center of puppet frame—he pats it)* ass is too big for a moped.

JUNE: *(Winds up for a punch)* Your ego's too big for a husband.

DR GOON: *(Also winds up for a punch)* You're gonna get it. You're really gonna get it. *(Whines and slowly sinks to knees)* How do you expect me to do well in the operating room when you put me down all the time? *(Crawls back and forth, looking up over puppet frame now and then)*

JUNE: I'm not putting you down. I'm defending myself. *(Looks around)* I can't even find you to put you down. You charge around all the time, and when you're not charging around, you're buried in a book like some catatonic.

DR GOON: *(Feverishly)* I have to study. I have to keep up. I have to save lives. Thank God, I can. Thank God, I can get some satisfaction at work. Between you and your insane children it's all I can do to keep my head above water. If you're not too tired, *(Mocks her voice talking into a telephone)* you're on the telephone with your hairdresser. You have to talk to your hairdresser because you don't have any friends.

(Puppet frame is removed. They resume former voices.)

ACT ONE

DR GOON: I don't know what's the matter with you. In our whole married life, we've never been able to make friends. And it's got to be *your* fault, because everyone is absolutely peachy to me at the hospital. *(He starts around.)*

JUNE: *(To* DR GOON's *back)* They have to be peachy to you. You're the "*M.* Deity!" We haven't been able to make any friends *(Twirls around, sits, gets her butt stuck in toy box)* because we move around so much. *(*JUNE *tries for the next three speeches to free herself.)*

DR GOON: *(Lovingly)* We're going to be here two whole years. If it wasn't for my brains in buying real estate, we wouldn't be able to pay for the kids' private schools. *(A promise)* We'll double our investment on this place when we sell out and move to the Sun Belt.

JUNE: And after we move to the Sun Belt, you'll want to move to the Snow Belt. I'm surprised we didn't move to Colorado. Look at all the skiing accidents.

DR GOON: *(Kneels—to himself)* I-80 is still more productive, and it'll be a bonanza when those dummies raise the speed limit. *(Frantically)* I just need two more years near a freeway, and then *(Crosses to* JUNE, *embraces her)* we can buy a castle in the Snow Belt and a villa in the Sun Belt.

JUNE: *(Aside)* I'd settle for "below" the belt. *(To* DR GOON*)* Now look who's talking about money.

DR GOON: *(On his feet)* I'm not talking about money, I'm talking about staying even. I'm talking about preserving *(Slaps her on these words)* what little capital we have left.

JUNE: I'm tired of this talk.

DR GOON: *(Turns away)* You're tired, period!

JUNE: I'm worn out.

DR GOON: I'll say you're worn out. *(Grabs* JUNE *by ankles)* Maybe you need a little tightening operation on your "love canal." *(Knocks her over on back—she's still in toy box.)*

JUNE: *(Kicking her feet)* You don't scare me.

DR GOON: *(Self-pity)* You don't know me.

JUNE: Don't make me throw up!

DR GOON: *(Grabs* JUNE's *hands, pulls her to sitting position)* When are you going to grow up? *(Picks up soft-sculpture* Physicians Desk Reference *and reads)*

JUNE: I believed you had an artistic soul once. *(Struggles, gets out of toy box, crosses to* DR GOON*)* That's how you got me to work for you.

DR GOON: *(Stuffs book under arm)* Wait a minute. I work for you. Do you think I want to work eighteen hours a day and be on call the other six? Is it my fault I'm the only one who can get patients in and out alive at a profit?

JUNE: *(Creeps up to* DR GOON, *tries to make up to him)* I am going to sleep for two days, and I want you to get someone to take care of the kids. I promise that when I wake up, I'll unpack, redecorate, and make the place a credit to your status, but moving makes me sick. *(Crosses)* We've moved so often that I feel totally rootless. You didn't notice that I cried the whole time we were moving. You didn't see how I felt about leaving that town. I'll admit we didn't have any friends, but I was attached to the lawn and the shrubs.

DR GOON: *(Exhausted by their exchange)* You're completely nuts.

JUNE: I don't think anybody will give us a chance to be friends. We can't be good friends.

DR GOON: Of course we can. If you'd just try.

JUNE: People don't want to get attached to us. They know we're just going to be moving on.

DR GOON: *(Rants, paces around stage)* That's a lily-livered, unChristian-like excuse for your own reclusive behavior. You hate people! You've driven our little girl so crazy that we have to chain her. That's why I don't want any friends. They'd have to see what a failure of a mother you are.

(JUNE, emotionally spent, falls asleep.)

DR GOON: *(Shaking and slapping her face)* Oh no you don't! *(Looks in JUNE's mouth. She snores in his face.)* What'd you take? My Quaaludes? Come back here. You're not going to leave me alone in this mess. *(Throws JUNE to floor)* Why can't you drink scotch like *(Kicks JUNE's behind)* normal people??? (DR GOON *exits.)*

(JUNE wakes up, stretches.)

JUNE: *(To audience)* Hello! *(Sings)*
I have a Jacuzzi,
An enclosed swimming pool,
Three children who will grow up perfectly.
My husband's a doctor,
I'm nobody's fool,
My property's worth four hundred-thousand dollars
And I'm happier than you, happier than you,
Happier than you!

(JUNE falls back onto the floor, asleep and snoring.)

(Lights up on the MARRIOTS. We see them through the up-center window.)

MRS MARRIOT: I'm worried.

MR MARRIOT: What else is new? *(Playfully hits MRS MARRIOT with a rolled-up soft-sculpture newspaper and turns away)*

MRS MARRIOT: I mean I'm worried about the people next door.

MR MARRIOT: Them? They got money. *(Turns, looks through window toward the* GOON *house)* He drives a Lincoln.

MRS MARRIOT: I'm not worrying about them starving.

MR MARRIOT: *(Puts arms around her)* What are you worried about?

MRS MARRIOT: The children.

MR MARRIOT: Who isn't worried about the children? I'm worried they'll wreck my lawn.

MRS MARRIOT: No, those children are well-behaved. Too well-behaved—outside, that is.

MR MARRIOT: *(Accusing)* Have you been staying up nights again?

MRS MARRIOT: Now, don't start with me. It isn't the change of life.

MR MARRIOT: *(Romantically)* I'm sorry dear. It's just that I've noticed when you don't get enough sleep the littlest things get you worried.

MRS MARRIOT: I was sound asleep last night. *(Shakes him off)* But screaming woke me up.

MR MARRIOT: You know it might have been a dream.

MRS MARRIOT: It wasn't a dream. It was children screaming.

MR MARRIOT: It could have been children playing. You know how kids love to scare each other.

MRS MARRIOT: At three in the morning?

MR MARRIOT: Maybe it was the late, late horror show. *(Transforms into a monster)* Dr. Frankenstein.

ACT ONE

MRS MARRIOT: It was the children next door. You know what sensitive ears I have. I know the tone in people's voices.

MR MARRIOT: You do admit you were asleep?

MRS MARRIOT: Of course, I was asleep. I told you I was asleep. If there's anything I can't abide it's to think of children or dogs being hurt.

MR MARRIOT: Especially dogs. *(With eye on* GOON *house)* Those people are really nice people. He's got a big job at the hospital. Put your mind on something positive like getting rid of the dandelions on our parking strip.

MRS MARRIOT: I know in my bones something isn't right over there at that house.

MR MARRIOT: *(Puts hands on her shoulders)* Now I'm getting worried about you. You mind your own business. *(Hold for a beat)*

(Lights down on MARRIOTS*)*

DR GOON: *(Struts onto the stage, singing to audience)*
I live in Omaha West
My house is newer than new,
I drive a Lincoln Continental
Painted Regency Blue.
I'm a super, super surgeon....
I eat caviar from sturgeon,
And I'm happier than you
Yeah, bet I'm happier than you, you, you!
Yeah, I'm happier than you, happier than you,
Happier than you or you or you.... YEAH!

*(*DR GOON *crosses to top of cat-tree; he is thinking in his study. He gathers in thought waves by reaching out the full extension of his arms and bringing his hands back to his forehead.* GAGA *skips in, stands center, in front of cat-tree.)*

GAGA: Dad, what's the difference between fission and fusion?

DR GOON: Na-a-a-a-a— *(GAGA ducks.)*

GAGA: Dad, what's the difference between fission and fusion?

DR GOON: Ask your mother, I'm busy.

GAGA: She isn't home yet.

DR GOON: I'm studying for an operation.

GAGA: You're so smart, Dad, that's why I'm asking you.

DR GOON: I have to put a stainless steel knee into a seventy-one-year-old leg tomorrow morning and I've never done it before. *(Jumps down onto floor)*

GAGA: *(Helps DR GOON up)* You can do it, Dad, you can do it. You put in a hip before, you put joints in fingers, you....

DR GOON: Go play in traffic.

GAGA: There isn't any.

DR GOON: *(Raises hand to hit GAGA)* What?

GAGA: *(Ducks, protects head)* Rush hour's over.

DR GOON: *(Embraces GAGA; they cross to teeter-totter)* Play with your brother.

GAGA: He can't move.

DR GOON: Why not?

GAGA: Don't you remember, he just came home from the hospital.

DR GOON: *(Moves away)* I'm a busy man, I can't be expected to remember everything.

GAGA: What's the difference between....

ACT ONE 13

DR GOON: One more sound and you go to bed.

GAGA: But Dad...I...

DR GOON: *(Bopping* GAGA*)* I have to study. Don't you have any homework to do?

GAGA: I finished.

DR GOON: *(Grabs* GAGA *by hair)* Why do you always finish your homework before I do? *(Puts other hand under chin)* I have to sweat over every word and you never seem to crack a book. Where'd you get your brains?

GAGA: I thought I got them from you, Dad.

DR GOON: *(Smacks* GAGA*)* Yap, yap, yap, you got them from your brother. Yap, yap *(Flips* GAGA*)* yap. I don't know why I have to be a crummy body mechanic. All I ever wanted to be was a poet. I am a poet. All these busted and broken-down *(Twists her ear)* muscles and bones and pesky cartilage are always interfering with my finer feelings. *(Flips* GAGA*)* If I could just earn enough money, I'd sleep for a month and then I'd buy a gross of pens with my name imprinted on them and I'll write beauty. *(Grabs* GAGA *by neck)* Sheer beauty. All I live for is the taste of air on my eyelids and the shadow of peach trees on my inner thighs, (GAGA *is down;* DR GOON *beats on her.)* a mud bath for my finger prints, a tent of robin's egg shells for my steaming sensual sensibility. I'm not God's repairman! I'm sensitive and my inner man is suffering from plastic molds of carcinogenic saccharin. I can build a stainless steel and cement back cast as well as Frank Lloyd Wright. But I'm sick of never sleeping, and I wake up screaming in the operating room *(Collars* GAGA; *drags her)* just as I wheel my patient up to my scalpel. *(Drops* GAGA*)* My scalpel, sharp and gleaming. I look deep into the mirror blade and pray, Dear God, don't ever make me have to shave my sensitive face again. I fall in love for a moment with my boyish grin, *(Drags* GAGA *by leg)* and tape the tractor-mangled toes of a teenage farm boy and transplant—from his ankle down — the leg of a frog. When this boy recovers, when he looks into the mirror to admire my handiwork, he will *(He leaps around the stage.)* leap from his anesthetic sleep as high as Baryshnikov! No workaholic can out-pace me! I'm dedicated with all my might to mending the fools who bash themselves to bits in their toy atomic roadsters, Caterpillar earth movers, and Cuisinart human-juicy-burger-makers. I have spent more time picking Plexiglas shrapnel out of pregnant hands and possible arms than any toothpick manufacturer. I'm not afraid of work! Someday I'm going to lay right down beside my work *(*GAGA *crawls away from* DR GOON, *who sits on teeter-totter.)* and take all the Demerol those lucky patients have guzzled. Then I'll go to sleep and write the portrait of my art. *(Sings)* "How I farted my life away...." *(Speaking)* sweating over picture books of new joints for mashed football bones. The maimed and the lame demand my delicate hands, *(Wrestling hold on* GAGA's *neck)* and I give my hands and mind to them for all their Blue Cross money, *(Drags* GAGA*)* while the Missouri rises above the flood plain and drowns my hospital in raw sewage. *(Releases her)* Yes—I, too, have learned to find beauty in this toxic garbage dump. That's the lesson we were meant to learn from non-biodegradable Pampers! *(Pulls* GAGA *up and embraces her; she struggles.)*

GAGA: Don't hurt me. Why do you hurt me when I love you, Daddy?

DR GOON: That cop gave me a speeding ticket. I'm a doctor. I'm immune to tickets.

ACT ONE 15

GAGA: *(Snuggles)* I love you, Daddy. I'll give you a vaccination. Roll up your sleeve.

DR GOON: A vaccination?

GAGA: Against speeding.

DR GOON: Speed? Yeah, yeah. Thanks, kid.

(He goes to medicine cabinet filled with soft sculpture pill bottles and a giant syringe...opens cabinet, takes out syringe, and rolls up sleeve; prepares to shoot up.)

GAGA: Daddy, Daddy! I want to do it. I want to do it for you.

DR GOON: *(Hears something)* Get out of the house.

GAGA: Let me! Let me!

DR GOON: Get out of the house. Your mother's driving up the drive.

GAGA: Can I have a towel to wipe off the blood?

DR GOON: What blood?

GAGA: Where you hit me.

DR GOON: *(Shoots up. The speed he injects takes effect; from here to end of the scene* DR GOON's *actions and speech are in triple time.)* I didn't hit you. Go out the back way and wait till your mother's inside. Then you come in the front door.

GAGA: My blood's on the floor.

DR GOON: *(Mopping floor with paper towel)* I'll get it up. You go on now.

GAGA: What'll I tell Mom?

DR GOON: Tell her you fell off the bars practicing gymnastics.

GAGA: She'll never believe me. It's after eight o'clock at night.

DR GOON: She don't know what time it is, she's too tired. Get going. Make something up. You got an I.Q. of a hundred and seventy-two.

GAGA: I'll do it on one condition.

DR GOON: What?

GAGA: What's the difference between fusion and fission?

DR GOON: Fission you do with a line and a pole, and fusion is when I mash your head with a baseball bat.

GAGA: Thanks, I think.

DR GOON: Get going. When you come back in I'll play Doctor with you.

GAGA: Oh, yippee! Yippee! Can I have some candy pills?

DR GOON: If you do everything like I told you. *(Grabbing her)* I didn't hit you, did I?

(Lights up on the MARRIOTS)

MRS MARRIOT: I know where to phone if people are hurting animals.

MR MARRIOT: *(Looks over paper)* It's none of your business.

MRS MARRIOT: Then you heard it, too. Admit it.

MR MARRIOT: *(Holds hand up in surrender)* I admit nothing.

MRS MARRIOT: What does a person do if children are being hurt?

MR MARRIOT: *(Grabs MRS MARRIOT's nose)* You keep your nose out of it. They aren't your children.

MRS MARRIOT: We're all God's children.

ACT ONE

MR MARRIOT: We don't have jurisdiction over other people's children.

MRS MARRIOT: I wonder if I could ask the police?

MR MARRIOT: We have to live in this neighborhood.

MRS MARRIOT: That's what I mean. I can't sit here and watch small children being hurt by adults.

MR MARRIOT: *(Nose to nose with* MRS MARRIOT*)* You don't know what's really going on. *(Looks toward* GOON *house)* The children did something to deserve it.

MRS MARRIOT: Then you did hear what I've been hearing.

MR MARRIOT: The wife must be on the angry side. No wonder, too. That poor husband of hers must work twenty hours a day.

MRS MARRIOT: You think she's beating them?

MR MARRIOT: *(Mimics wife)* Well, I can't see him doing it. He's a doctor.

MRS MARRIOT: Yes, he is!

MR MARRIOT: Besides, a man's home is his castle. What goes on behind closed doors is no concern of ours.

MRS MARRIOT: But the screams! Those blood-curdling screams! And those screams aren't always kids' screams either.

MR MARRIOT: Ah, the wife's probably going crazy from being alone with kids so much.

MRS MARRIOT: Why do you think it's the wife?
(Hits MR MARRIOT *on the head with his newspaper)*

*(*JUNE, GAGA, *and* GARFIELD *are on stage.* DR GOON *enters, wearing a bloody lab coat.)*

DR GOON: Anybody home?

CHILDREN: *(Jumping all over him)* Daddy, Daddy. You got home before dark.

DR GOON: It's the first time in a month.

JUNE: *(Crosses to DR GOON)* Dinner's ready! It's just right. Succulent and full of juice. You'll have a good dinner for a change.

DR GOON: Bring me my lounge coat. *(With a grand gesture, he accidentally backhands JUNE; she spins, then goes to bring coat.)*

JUNE: *(Helps him out of bloody white coat and into clean replica of coat)* What a treat to have you home early. Maybe we can even play croquet after dinner.

DR GOON: Sounds good.

(GARFIELD and GAGA cross to teeter-totter, sniffling and wiping noses and eyes.)

GARFIELD: We had so much fun at school today.

GAGA: We played on the playground and rolled in the grass.

DR GOON: *(Moves to CHILDREN)* Why are you snuffling?

CHILDREN: Are we?

DR GOON: Are you sick again?

CHILDREN: No. We feel good. We feel fine.

DR GOON: Your eyes are red.

GAGA: They are? They don't want to be. Maybe it's a little sunburn. The sun was out, wasn't it?

JUNE: They've just been having fun for a change. They're making new friends.

DR GOON: *(Moves closer to twist JUNE's ear)* I'm glad they can make friends. That's more than you can do.

ACT ONE

(Both CHILDREN *run to divert and hug* DR GOON.*)*

GARFIELD: We haven't seen you for so long, Daddy.

GAGA: You don't get home till we're in bed.

DR GOON: Daddy has to work hard to save lives.

GAGA: You're so strong, Dad. I want to hug you.

DR GOON: O.K. *(Notices their hands)* Oh, God. My coat. Don't touch me! You're filthy! Dirty!

CHILDREN: We just love you, Daddy.

(Actor playing SINK *enters and remains through the scene. The* SINK, *through facial gesture, reinforces* DR GOON's *tyrannical point of view. Two* VISITING NURSES *enter and hold puppet frame so that all action at the teeter-totter is framed by the puppet frame.)*

DR GOON: Come here to the sink, children.

*(*CHILDREN *behind teeter-totter wash hands in* SINK.*)*

JUNE: *(Running into room)* Dinner's ready, everyone.

DR GOON: *(Moves from behind frame—he and* JUNE *collide belly to belly;* JUNE *falls.)* Hold the dinner. I'm teaching the kids to scrub.

JUNE: They washed their hands, dear.

DR GOON: Not enough. *(Pulling* JUNE *to her feet by her hair)* Their nails are dirty. I'm sick of them always whining. They whine because their noses and eyes are runny and their throats are always sore. Sick kids whine, of course they do. *(Slaps* JUNE*)* I hit upon the reason! They don't keep clean enough to kill the germs. I brought green soap home from the hospital. Put out your hands, children. *(Crosses behind puppet frame)*

JUNE: *(Crosses behind puppet frame and pleads)*
The dinner will dry out.

DR GOON: Add water.

JUNE: It's not that kind of food. It's perfect, now.

DR GOON: *(Pulls* JUNE *up by her ears)* I'm teaching now! *(Pops* JUNE *on head)* Use your brains if you have any.

GARFIELD: What about Gogo, can she wash her hands?

DR GOON: *(Arms around* GAGA *and* GARFIELD*)* You know we can't let her loose. But when you're clean you can take a basin over to her, and we'll each scrub a paw. Cleanliness will improve a lot of things around here.

JUNE: But everything is clean. This is a brand new house.

DR GOON: And it's going to stay that way. When we move I want to get my money out of it. Scrub like this. *(*SINK *hisses as he demonstrates surgical scrub, and* CHILDREN *follow him.)* Soap like this, rinse like this, scrub like this.

CHILDREN: Like this, Daddy? Like this?

DR GOON: Like that, but harder. Get that dirt out from under your fingernails. *(Moves to in front of puppet frame)* Use that brush.

JUNE: *(Crosses to* DR GOON*)* Hey, that's my vegetable brush.

DR GOON: So what.

JUNE: Talk about germs. You'll get my vegetable brush dirty.

DR GOON: *(*JUNE *shrinks as he speaks.)* Buy another one! I make enough money to afford two vegetable brushes. *(Grabs* JUNE *by collar and throws her against wall. She falls asleep.)* Get back to the food. If it's burnt, you'll eat it and I'll take the kids out to dinner.

ACT ONE 21

(After witnessing DR GOON's *violent treatment of* JUNE, GAGA *and* GARFIELD *transform into Incredible Hulk-like monsters and go through the puppet frame. They make monster sounds and lift* DR GOON *over their heads.* DR GOON *quickly gives them a shot from a hypodermic to calm them down.)*

CHILDREN: *(Referring to* SINK*)* Spray us with water, Daddy. We're hot.

*(*JUNE *comes to in kitchen, stage right.)*

DR GOON: I didn't do that for fun. You scrub, now. You're learning how we do it at the hospital. O.K. *(He chants like a football cheer.)* Kill those germs! Save those lives! Kill those germs! Clean those hands! Where have your hands been? All day long in touch with dirt. All day long in touch with the germs of dirty kids at school. Everything you touch clings to you. Wash it off. Wash it off so you can put clean food in your mouth.

JUNE: *(Exasperated, she bangs pots and pans. She enters the scene carrying a soft sculpture burnt cow on a tray.)* I'll start all over. This dinner's ruined.

DR GOON: *(To* CHILDREN*)* O.K. That's a good start. Let's eat.

JUNE: Keep scrubbing. I'm going to make a new dinner. *(Starts to leave)*

DR GOON: That's the way I love roast. You make it too rare. I see enough blood in the operating room.

JUNE: But it has no food value left!

DR GOON: I'm the doctor here. I'll be the judge of that. *(He signals* JUNE *to serve. The teeter-totter has become the dinner table.)* Sit down children. Hold up your hands, first. There, see that? Look at that. Aren't they clean?

JUNE: *(Looks at* CHILDREN's *hands)* The skin's peeling off their fingers.

DR GOON: It'll grow back. The longer I'm in the medical profession the more I marvel at the recovery power of the human body.

(GARFIELD *snatches cow and begins to chew on it.)*

GARFIELD: It's fun to gnaw on bones.

*(*DR GOON *backhands him; he flies off chair.* JUNE *runs to* GARFIELD.*)*

GARFIELD: *(Holds up hands)* But my hands are clean. Look. I did what you said.

DR GOON: My kids don't eat like animals.

*(*JUNE *and* DR GOON *help* GARFIELD *up.* JUNE *takes her place opposite* DR GOON *at the table.)*

JUNE: He was just trying to gnaw the meat. It's too dried out to cut.

DR GOON: Is this the kind of table manners you taught my children? Oh, by the way, you said you needed a little help around the house. Well, guess what? Have I got a surprise for you! My mother's consented to join us, and teach you how to do things right.

JUNE: Not Mother Goon! *(She falls asleep.)*

DR GOON: You asked for help and you're going to get it. *(As a coach to the* CHILDREN*)* You children are Goons! Don't you ever forget it! *(Kicks* GARFIELD's *feet out from under him; he falls to floor.)* Goons sit up at table and eat with knives and forks. Goons are not animals. *(Pulls him up)* Get back in your chair and act like you know you're from a great family. You're a Goon. Who are you?

GARFIELD: *(Whimpering)* I don't know.

ACT ONE

DR GOON: You know who you are. *(Slaps him)* Who are you?

GARFIELD: I'm Garfield.

DR GOON: Who?

GARFIELD: I don't want to be like you.

DR GOON: *(Holds* GARFIELD *to his chest)* You're mine and you're a Goon. *(Slaps* GARFIELD *on back)* Act like a Goon. Who are you?

GARFIELD: I'm Garfield Goon.

DR GOON: Who are you?

GARFIELD: *(Through tears)* Goon.

DR GOON: I can't hear you through that pansy-assed blubbering. Who are you?

GARFIELD: Goon. I'm a Goon!

(DR GOON *slaps* GARFIELD *firmly on his back.* GARFIELD *flips over teeter-totter.* GAGA *and* JUNE *come downstage, whimpering.)*

DR GOON: Goons are men! Sit up and act like a man. Someday you'll have to run things. Act like a man! Who are you?

JUNE & CHILDREN: *(Face the audience)* Goons!

(GOON *family exits.)*

(The VISITING NURSES *enter and sing:)*

SONG OF THE VISITING NURSES

We are the Visiting Nurses,
We're the Flying V's,
We work one-on-one,
Dealing with everything from mental disease,
To the loneliness of age, to skinned knees.

We are the Flying V's,
Stronger than anyone knows—
We're ordinary Wonder Women, *(Solo)* and men,
In our navy blue and white clothes.

We may get tired but we're never bored
Because we know
Deep in our hearts,
Virtue is its own re—
Virtue is its own re—
Virtue is its own reward!

(VISITING NURSES walk to imaginary door in a line, an arm on shoulder of the person in front.)

NURSE 3: Have you spent your lives in our profession?

NURSE 1: We're not that old.

NURSE 2: We're not quite as old as we feel.

(They have arrived at imaginary door. They give NURSE 3 the honor of ringing.)

NURSE 3: I'm sorry. I didn't mean to get into age—it's just I love people, *(Rings bell)* and to get paid for helping people is my idea of heaven. *(Rings bell)*

NURSE 2: I know what you mean.

NURSE 1: *(Knocks on door)* It's great to help a new mother learn to care for her baby.

NURSE 3: Mothers don't know how to care for a baby?

NURSE 2: Many do.

NURSE 1: Some don't even love their new babies.

NURSE 3: I never heard of such a thing.

NURSE 2: Some of the younger ones look at the newborn and say, "Who are you?"

NURSE 1: You can help them get into their kids, by teaching them how to care for it. *(Knocks again on door)*

ACT ONE 25

Somehow, caring for another human being, and watching it grow and change can help kindle love in a new mother.

NURSE 2: *(Sotto voce)* Or more hate.

NURSE 3: Gee, I thought mother love was automatic.

VISITING NURSES 1 and 2: *(Laugh)* You've got a lot to learn.
(The VISITING NURSES leave imaginary door and get back into their van [The teeter-totter.])
We're the Visiting Nurses
We're the Flying V's,
Our bedside manner is warm,
Our home address is a mystery,
We are stronger than anyone knows—
We're ordinary Wonder Women, *(Solo)* and men,
In our navy blue and white clothes
(Solo) Powder blue in summer.

We may get tired,
But we're never bored
Because we know—
....
Virtue is its own re—
Virtue is its own re—
Virtue is its own reward!

(VISITING NURSES pump up and down on teeter-totter as if driving in their van. VISITING NURSES 1 and 2 on ends of teeter-totter, #3 in middle. All face front. Pumping slows, then stops.)

NURSE 1: Out of gas! Would you mind pushing?

NURSE 3: *(Gallantly gets out, starts pushing)* Do you think we'll have trouble getting respect from people?

NURSE 1: *(Teeter-totter starts going again)* You respect people and they'll respect you.

NURSE 3: But I mean, like, cops get instant respect. Do we have to prove ourselves first?

NURSE 2: I don't mind proving myself.

NURSE 1: We have even more clout than cops.

NURSE 3: You're kidding. *(Runs and jumps on teeter-totter)*

NURSE 2: I believe that, but does the public?

NURSE 1: The paper took this poll and, to the public, nurses now have more status than teachers or cops, but not as much as lawyers.

NURSE 3: Or "M. Deities."

VISITING NURSES 1 and 2: *(Cover his mouth with their hands)* You can bet on it!

(VISITING NURSES exit.)

GOON CHILDREN: *(Enter and sing, directly to audience)*

HAPPIER THAN YOU

My Daddy is a handsome, nervous doctor.
I'm nervy, too.
My mommy is beautiful and neurotic.
I'm beautiful, too.
Our phone number is unlisted
So we don't have to talk to anyone new
I have a gifted, genius I.Q....
I go to a private grade school,
And I'm happier than you,
Yes, I'm happier than you and
you and you and you and you
Yes, I'm happier than you and
you and you and you and you and you!
NYAAHH!

(As more lights come up, JUNE *is seen passed-out on the teeter-totter.* GOGO *is chained to cat-tree.* GAGA *and* GARFIELD *encircle* JUNE.*)*

GAGA: Mommy?

JUNE: *(Sleepily)* Yes?

GARFIELD: Are you awake?

JUNE: Mmmmmm?

GAGA: *(Into* JUNE's *ear)* Are you awake? *(Crawls onto teeter-totter)*

JUNE: Is Daddy home?

GARFIELD: *(Jumps on teeter-totter)* Daddy phoned, he had to work all night.

GAGA: *(Playfully yelling)* Are you awake?

JUNE: Dad has to work?

GARFIELD: Yes.

JUNE: *(Pops up; they start to teeter-totter.)* Then I'm awake.

GAGA: Are we going to stay in our new house?

JUNE: We are staying in it.

GAGA: I mean, are we going to stay here now, forever and ever?

JUNE: I sure hope so.

GOGO: EEEEEEEEEEEEEOOOOOOOOOOOO HIHIHIHIHIHIHIHIH!

JUNE: *(To* GOGO*)* Are you happy here?

GOGO: Yip yip yip yip yip!

JUNE: I think she's happy here.

*(*CHILDREN *cross to* JUNE.*)*

GARFIELD: Can we put her in her romper swing?

(During next section of dialogue, they pull down and prepare romper swing.)

JUNE: Why not?

GAGA: Was she always like that?

JUNE: No, she was worse.

GARFIELD: Why?

JUNE: I don't know.

GAGA: We're not that way.

GARFIELD: Why aren't we?

GAGA: Why aren't we, Mom, why?

JUNE: Because you're not.

GARFIELD: But why?

JUNE: If I knew, I'd help her not to be that way.

GAGA: But she likes being that way.

JUNE: *(Goes to GAGA)* No she doesn't, she wants to be like you.

GARFIELD: How do you know?

JUNE: *(Crosses to GARFIELD)* Why, anyone would want to be like you. You're good, and sweet, and you help Mommy all you can.

GAGA: She looks happy, Mommy, not just today, but most of the time.

JUNE: *(Moves to GAGA and strokes her; GARFIELD crosses to GOGO.)* How do you know she's happy?

GARFIELD: *(Playfully—as if for GOGO's amusement—he jumps and rolls over teeter-totter.)* She smiles and laughs, and throws things and laughs and jumps and

ACT ONE

laughs. *(Grabs* GAGA *by the hand; they cross to* GOGO, *unchain her, and put her in romper swing.)*

*(*JUNE *begins remembering; she moves downstage center.)*

JUNE: She might be in pain when she laughs. When you were little babies and you laughed, people thought you were happy too, but I knew you really had gas, and the pain made your face look like a laugh.

GAGA: *(Crosses to one side of* JUNE*)* Why?

JUNE: Because that's the way God made them, that's why.

GAGA: Did God make Gogo that way?

JUNE: *(To herself)* I'm not too sure. It must have been God, but if it wasn't God, who might have made her that way?

GAGA: I know. *(Whispers in* JUNE's *ear)*

GARFIELD: *(Jumps up and down, tugging at* JUNE*)* Tell me, too! Tell me, too!

*(*GOGO *throws something at them.)*

JUNE: She knows we're talking about her. *(*JUNE *blows a kiss.)* We love you.

GAGA: I think Daddy made her that way.

JUNE: Now, now, that's not nice to say.

GAGA: It wasn't nice to do.

GARFIELD: I don't know. She gets anything she wants, and she doesn't have to do any work.

GAGA: I'd rather be me than chained to a cat-tree.

GARFIELD: What happened to our cats?

JUNE: Daddy thought they were too dirty so he sent them away.

GARFIELD: Where?

JUNE: To a little town called Euthanasia.

GARFIELD: Where's that?

JUNE: On the Missouri side of Kansas City.

GARFIELD: Can we go out and play?

JUNE: It's raining.

GAGA: *(Throws tantrum)* Why?

JUNE: We just put Gogo in her romper swing.

GARFIELD: Why?

JUNE: You wanted to.

GAGA: Now we want to all go out and play.

JUNE: It's too wet.

GARFIELD: Why?

JUNE: The rain comes out of the sky and makes the ground wet.

GAGA: *(Shows sneakers)* I have my sneakers on.

JUNE: Your sneakers can get wet.

GARFIELD: And they can get dry.

JUNE: But they'll fall apart if they get wet.

GAGA & GARFIELD: Why?

(All the "why's" and questions about Daddy are building to drive JUNE over the edge.)

JUNE: *(Pleading)* Because they don't make 'em like they used to.

GAGA & GARFIELD: *(Turn to JUNE and yell)* Why?

JUNE: That's what I'd like to know.

(JUNE begins to pass out. CHILDREN catch her, take her hands, and swing them together, as they remember.)

ACT ONE

WHEN I WAS A LITTLE GIRL

(Note to Director: In this song a line is sung and then the action is performed, and so on. As JUNE *remembers the past in this song, she unconsciously hurts the* CHILDREN *with her actions: e.g., 1. A playful hand swing becomes a flip; 2. a gesture as* JUNE *opens her arms—back-hands* GAGA.*)*

JUNE: *(Sings)* When I was a little girl
(Flips GARFIELD*)*
Sneakers were strong,
(Crosses to GARFIELD, *concerned)*
A sucker lasted all day long.
(Slaps GAGA, *then looks after her)*

(CHILDREN *transform into super-heroes.)*

JUNE: When I was a child
Everyone loved children,
What's gone wrong?
Oh, my honey, why?

When I was a little girl
Songs had melody,
When I was a little girl
Bread tasted good
Even without honey.

When I was a child

(CHILDREN *transform into comic book characters.)*

JUNE: Everyone loved children
Donald Duck was really funny,
What's gone wrong?
Oh, my honey, why?

*(*GARFIELD *and* GOGO *grip* JUNE's *hands and ankles and swing her.* GAGA *pushes from behind.)*

CHILDREN: *(Sing)* Don't be sad, Mommy
We have a new home now.

(CHILDREN set JUNE on floor, tickle her.)

CHILDREN: We don't have to start over again;
You said this time, this time, this time,
We'd get to be glad!

GOONA-GOONA

JUNE: *(Sings)* Oh, I love you,
(ALL embrace as in a warm family portrait)
Your face is like the moona.
(She flips and becomes disoriented.)
Who are you?
And where do you belong?
I'm a Goon, a Goona-Goon.

(With GAGA on one far side of the stage and GARFIELD on the other, they take turns throwing GOGO [flipping her] from stage right to left.)

(JUNE walks zombielike up one side and down the other of the teeter-totter.)

ALL: Goona goona, Goona goona
Goona goona, Goona goona!
I'd just as soona love a tuna—as
Love you Goona!
You make me swoona, you Goona Goons!
Goona, goona, goona, goona—goo-na!
Goona, goona, goona, goona—goo-na!
Goona, goona, goona, goona, goona, goona
Goona Goons—
Love you, Goona!

JUNE: I love you as big as the moona
All of you, you Goona Goons.

(JUNE passes out.)

CHILDREN: Goona, goona, goona, goona, goo-na!
Goona, goona, goona, goona, goo-na!
Goona, goona, goona, goona, goona, goona

ACT ONE

Goona, Goons—
Love you Goona!

          END OF ACT ONE

ACT TWO

(Lights up on DR GOON *and* MRS MARRIOT. *Each is watering their lawn with a piece of colored plastic tubing.)*

DR GOON: That's a beautiful lawn you have there, Mrs. Marriot.

MRS MARRIOT: Thank you, Doctor.

DR GOON: I'm good with my hands, but only with human beings.

MRS MARRIOT: I beg your pardon, Doctor?

DR GOON: On the operating table. I'm good there. I don't seem to have a green thumb.

MRS MARRIOT: It's just patience, I guess.

DR GOON: *(Moves closer to* MRS MARRIOT*)* Your lawn is bright green and my lawn is still dull. It looks dead. *(He lets garden hose go limp.)*

MRS MARRIOT: Give it plenty of water, Doctor, it'll green up then, I think. 'Peers to be Zoysia.

DR GOON: Zoysia? I don't know that disease.

MRS MARRIOT: You must be teasing me, Doctor.

DR GOON: I'm not. *(Moves closer to* MRS MARRIOT*)* But I might like to, Mrs. Marriot.

MRS MARRIOT: Zoysia is a species of grass, Doctor.

DR GOON: Why, thank you, Mrs. Marriot. I like to learn new things. That's why I like medicine.

MRS MARRIOT: Must be a fascinating life.

DR GOON: Demanding, too. This is the first afternoon I've had off in six years.

MRS MARRIOT: You must be an important man?

DR GOON: They can't do without me. I take good care of my hands. *(Moves behind MRS MARRIOT so he can get a feel in as he shows her his hands)* They're always ready. See? Take a look—insured by Lloyds of London for five million each.

MRS MARRIOT: *(Giggling)* They must be very knowing and skillful.

DR GOON: My patients think so. *(Passionately grabs her)* Would you like to join me on the patio for some *(Sings)* scotch and soda?...jigger of gin...?

MRS MARRIOT: *(Frees herself)* I'd love to, but may I have a rain check? It's my husband's birthday, and I'm fixing him his favorite dinner.

DR GOON: *(Grabs MRS MARRIOT around knees)* You're my idea of a perfect wife.

MRS MARRIOT: Thank you, Doctor. 'Bye, now.

(They exit.)

(GAGA and GARFIELD on teeter-totter; GOGO is chained to cat-tree.)

GARFIELD: Are your hands grown back?

GAGA: Not hands, Garfield—skin!

GARFIELD: It's back—I missed it!

GAGA: Do you like Daddy?

GARFIELD: What do you mean by "like"?

GAGA: Do you feel better when he's at home or when he's at work?

ACT TWO

GARFIELD: When he's at work.

GAGA: Me, too.

GOGO: I'm going to *be* Daddy when I grow up.

GAGA: At the rate you're going, you aren't going to grow up.

GOGO: *(Holding up chained wrists)* I can't grow, if I'm like this all the time.

GARFIELD: It's for your own good.

GOGO: Chains are for my own good?

GAGA: *(Moves to GOGO)* You hurt yourself when you're free.

GARFIELD: *(Moves to GOGO)* You hurt us when you're free.

GOGO: I don't mean to.

GAGA: Why do you do it?

GOGO: Daddy does it.

GAGA & GARFIELD: *(Backs to audience, they hold hands and cover GOGO's mouth.)* Does what?

GOGO: Hurts people.

GAGA & GARFIELD: *(Turn front, still holding hands)* What people?

GOGO: *(Breaking their grip)* You think I don't know what goes on around here?

GARFIELD: Did you have your medicine today?

GOGO: Yes, *(Elbows GARFIELD in tummy)* dope, I did.

GAGA: You never talked this good before.

GOGO: I can talk if I feel like it.

GARFIELD: Mother will be so happy.

GOGO: I won't talk for her. *(Clenches her teeth)*

GAGA & GARFIELD: Why not?

GOGO: *(Through clenched teeth)* She let him chain me up.

GAGA & GARFIELD: But you bang your head on the refrigerator.

GOGO: *(Blaring, with hands to head)* You would, too, if your head hurt like mine!

GAGA & GARFIELD: Where does it hurt?

GOGO: All over my head, way deep inside my head, and it feels like grinding broken glass inside my eyes.

(During the following, GOGO gets very soft in order to get GAGA and GARFIELD's sympathy while they pet and calm her.)

GAGA & GARFIELD: All the time?

GOGO: All the time. Almost all.

GAGA: When doesn't it hurt?

GOGO: When I have my medicine, it still hurts, but not as bad.

GARFIELD: Why do you want to hurt us?

(GAGA and GARFIELD take GOGO through a slow flip over teeter-totter.)

GOGO: I can't help it. It hurts so much I want you to hurt, too. You have to hurt as much as I do.

(GAGA and GARFIELD run around teeter-totter and pull GOGO to her feet; they embrace her.)

GARFIELD: We feel sorry for you.

GOGO: *(Under her breath)* Dopes, stupid dopes.

GAGA: We do feel sorry for you.

ACT TWO

(We should see GOGO *struggling not to do the horrible things she feels like doing to her brother and sister. But viciousness comes through her voice loud and clear.)*

GOGO: Dopes, stupid dopes! Idiot toilet bowl brushes! Teeney weeney spiders! Little Miss Muffets! It doesn't do me any good for you to feel sorry for me. It doesn't make my head stop hurting. It doesn't get me out of my chains. How will I ever grow up? My bones are deformed, my body aches all over. Daddy Jack Horner only lets me out in the morning and the night to pee and to poop. *(Bounces* GAGA *and* GARFIELD *with her hips, one on "pee" and one on "poop")* That's the only exercise I ever get.

GAGA & GARFIELD: You get to eat.

GOGO: Mommie feeds me.

GARFIELD: She has to! You throw the food in her face and at the walls, and on Lorna, the dog.

*(*GOGO *acts out the grossness she describes.)*

GOGO: I hate that food. It's all yellow. If it isn't yellow, it's red, *(Terrorizes* GARFIELD*)* if it isn't red, it's blue, *(Terrorizes* GAGA—*shakes her)* if it isn't blue, it's green. *(*GOGO *crosses to center of teeter-totter.)* All the food is painted with poison, you dopes. Don't you know they're poisoning us to death? Don't you pay attention to the TV, don't you read the health news in the *Weird Herald*? You're all dying of cancer. Only the old will be around to enjoy the earth. The ones who still bake their own bread, and dig their own gardens. It's curtains for you, you feeling sorry, Nubian Goat, Mother Goslings!

GAGA: Are you sure you took your medicine today?

GOGO: Come over here, little boy blue, and look in my mouth. *(Sticks out her tongue)*

GAGA: Why?

GOGO: Because the dye from the pill is still on my tongue, Buggsie Bunny!

GAGA: That's not my name!

GOGO: *(Moves closer so she can better irritate GAGA)* What *is* your name? All I ever hear you called around here is "Shut up" or "Go to your room." Which do you like to be called, "Shut up" or "Go to your...?"

GAGA: *(Reacts violently; GARFIELD runs to restrain her)* You shut up talking to me that way!

GOGO: *(Prancing around)* I thought you ignorant toadstools were thrilled that I decided to talk at all.

GARFIELD: (GARFIELD *and* GAGA *climb up cat-tree.*) We are happy to hear you talking in a regular voice. You scared us most of the time before. You would just scream and roar. You are sometimes like an animal. *(He turns his back on GOGO, as does GAGA.)*

GOGO: (GOGO *grabs both by the hair; their heads dangle dangerously over the platform edge.*) I have news for you, Banbury Cross. Come here and listen to me. WE ARE ALL ANIMALS. BUT NOT AS BAD AS DADDY. HE'S A MONSTER!

GAGA & GARFIELD: *(Struggling)* He is not.

GOGO: He hits you. He hurts you. He hurts Mommy, he makes her cry. He beats me black and blue and chains me to this cat-tree. *(Releases* GAGA *and* GARFIELD; *pleads with them)* Let me out for five minutes? Just to stretch. Please? My blood is stopping up. Look how blue my arms are.

GAGA: You talk too mean.

GARFIELD: *(Bops* GOGO *on the head)* Daddy wouldn't like it.

ACT TWO

GOGO: Of course, he wouldn't like it. He'd kill you, if he found out you let me out. But he isn't going to know, unless you tell him. Is he?

GAGA & GARFIELD: *(They hug each other.)* What if he comes home?

GOGO: That workaholic will be at the hospital past midnight. You'll both be lucky if you get anything to eat.

GAGA & GARFIELD: We can cook.

GOGO: I wish you'd share some good food with me.

GAGA & GARFIELD: What?

GOGO: Oatmeal.

GAGA & GARFIELD: We don't know how to cook that.

GOGO: You don't know as much as you think you do, do you? I like it raw anyway. *(Marches around, full of herself)* Put some raisins in it and bring it here!

GAGA & GARFIELD: *(GAGA comes down cat-tree)* I guess that would be all right.

GOGO: *(As she plots, she slowly climbs cat-tree.)* Do you want to be my sister and brother, or do you want to be enemies of me?

GAGA & GARFIELD: We want to be.... I don't know.

GOGO: *(Petting GARFIELD)* Do you feel love for me?

GAGA & GARFIELD: You're our sister.

GOGO: But do you feel love, too? *(Twists GARFIELD's arm behind him)* Or do you just feel sorry? You Rat! You Mole!

GAGA & GARFIELD: We should love you.

GOGO: Throw out that word "should." Do you, or don't you? *(Throws GARFIELD off cat-tree)*

GAGA & GARFIELD: We love you.

GOGO: *(Reaches for* GARFIELD; *he helps her down. Then she throws him to floor.)* If you love me, do you want to make me happy? (GAGA *runs to help him.)*

GAGA & GARFIELD: I don't know.

GOGO: *(Wiggles in between* GAGA *and* GARFIELD) Are you sure you are my brother and my sister? Did God send two spiders to live with me, or did She send me a brother and a sister?

GAGA & GARFIELD: We want to make you happy

GOGO: *(Conspiratorial)* Get the key. Get the key. We'll play a great game of King of the Castle, if you let me free.

GARFIELD: I didn't know you knew any games.

GOGO: Just because I've been chained here by that monster you call Daddy doesn't mean I'm as stupid as you are.

GAGA: Mommie chained you, too. It's for your own good. *(Faces* GARFIELD. *They do mirror images of seeing self, then winding up for a punch. The image ends as they fall to the floor.)* Look at that horrible scar on your forehead. Look what you did to yourself when you got away.

GARFIELD: *(Looking over teeter-totter)* And you should have seen the refrigerator door. We had to get a new one. They couldn't even get any money on a trade-in. You broke it.

GOGO: I was very little then. I didn't know what I was doing. I thought the refrigerator was Daddy. I wanted to kill him.

(Mirror work ends.)

ACT TWO

GAGA & GARFIELD: *(Laughing)* You're funny. You're crazy. Daddy isn't a refrigerator.

GOGO: He isn't anymore. Now, he's a hospital.

GAGA & GARFIELD: *(Laughing)* He isn't a hospital.

GOGO: What's the difference? He thinks he is. *(Calling them closer)* Hey, get the key. Let's have fun. Come here and feel my face. Look into my eyes. You'll see how much I love you and that you can trust me. Get the key.

(GOGO *and* GARFIELD *go hesitantly to where* GOGO *is chained and look into her eyes. Slowly they feel her face.* GOGO *rubs her face on their hands.)*

GOGO: Oh, please? Let me out. Just for a little while? I promise to do anything you say. I do, I promise. I will do anything you say. I promise.

GAGA & GARFIELD: *You* will do anything *we* say?

GOGO: I love you. I promise.

GAGA & GARFIELD: *(Looking at each other)* Shall we? *(They nod.)* Get the key.

(GAGA *and* GARFIELD *get the key, unlock, and unchain* GOGO. GOGO *stretches, smiles, jumps up and down, and begins to tear the house apart. Lights dim and then flash and explode to punctuate the following action.)*

GOGO: I win! *(Chases* GAGA *and* GARFIELD, *beats them with chains)*

GAGA: Let's play that game!

GOGO: I already played a game with you.

GAGA & GARFIELD: We let you out.

GOGO: You didn't let me out. I let myself out by fooling you.

GARFIELD: You have to go back in five minutes.

GOGO: I'm free, I don't have to do anything.
(Chains up GARFIELD*)*

GAGA & GARFIELD: You promised.

GOGO: *(Grabs* GAGA, *drags her to teeter-totter, puts her head under one end, bangs teeter-totter on her head)* I did that to prove how stupid and dumb you are, Jack and Jill. I want to see you fall down the hill.

*(*GOGO *picks up bat and beats and slaps and kicks them.* GOGO *screams with laughter, as* GAGA *and* GARFIELD *scream in pain and betrayal.* GOGO *beats them until they can't fight back, then chains them together, beats them some more, then starts to demolish house, laughing wildly.* GOGO *stops now and then to beat her own head against the wall or the edge of the teeter-totter.)*

(The final image is of GOGO *placing her head under one end of the teeter-totter. As she crushes her own head under it four times she laughs hysterically.)*

(Lights up on MARRIOTS; *they are in bed.)*

MR MARRIOT: *(Eyes wide open)* That was a great dinner. *(Exercises)* Perfect, but I'm wide awake.

MRS MARRIOT: *(She turns over.)* Mmmmmmmmmm.

MR MARRIOT: Are you awake?

MRS MARRIOT: No.

MR MARRIOT: *(Puts arms around* MRS MARRIOT*)* I love you honey. Thanks for the meal.

MRS MARRIOT: Anytime.

MR MARRIOT: It was a great birthday, *(Looks through window toward* GOONS' *house)* except for that screaming from next door.

MRS MARRIOT: I don't think it was screaming.

ACT TWO

MR MARRIOT: Maybe we should call the Humane Society and see if they know what to do if people are mistreated. Somebody's beating somebody over there.

MRS MARRIOT: You're right. It's the late, late show.

MR MARRIOT: Those screams and sobs were real.

MRS MARRIOT: You're dreaming on your birthday cake. *(She snuggles in.)*

MR MARRIOT: That guy is beating his kids and maybe the wife, too. *(*MRS MARRIOT *is awake; she sits up.)*

MRS MARRIOT: That guy, as you call him, is the best surgeon in town.

MR MARRIOT: How do you know?

MRS MARRIOT: He told me. A man like that couldn't beat up on people. He's dedicated to save lives.

MR MARRIOT: Something's wrong over there!

MRS MARRIOT: It's our imagination. Those people have a lot of money. They probably have stereo television with rock-and-roll speakers. Come to sleep, honey. You have to get up early.

MR MARRIOT: I admit I thought you were going overboard at first. But now I'm calling the police! *(He reaches for the phone;* MRS MARRIOT *stops him.)*

MRS MARRIOT: You said the Humane Society.

MR MARRIOT: I can't take that screaming any more.

MRS MARRIOT: *(Seductively to* MR MARRIOT *as she looks through window toward* GOON *home)* I had a nice chat with the Doctor today, darling. I just can't believe that what I thought about him was possible for me to think. He's so charming, so kind, so nice!

MR MARRIOT: Look, I don't like to get involved in another man's family problems, but I'm going to check out his kids before that mini-bus picks them up for their school tomorrow.

MRS MARRIOT: What do you mean?

MR MARRIOT: I'm going to see that they're all in one piece!

MRS MARRIOT: Now look who's going overboard!

(In bed, they turn back to back.)

MRS MARRIOT: Hrummmmph!

MR MARRIOT: Hrummmmph!

(Lights up on GRANDMA GOON, *sitting on teeter-totter.* GARFIELD *and* GAGA *enter, laughing and tickling each other.)*

GRANDMA: Where have you been, children?

*(*GARFIELD *and* GAGA *stop and, in response to* GRANDMA's *voice, straighten up.)*

GARFIELD: Playing.

GRANDMA: With nice children?

GAGA: Yes, Grandma.

GRANDMA: *(Pulls* CHILDREN *to her, begins bouncing them on her knees)* With those lovely Porterhouse children?

CHILDREN: They're no fun.

GRANDMA: They're lots of fun. They're very well-behaved children. *(Throws* GARFIELD; *he tumbles downstage.)* Their father is president of Doctor's Insurance. Their mother was Panhellenic Princess and coordinates the alumni committee.

GAGA: Can we have some juice?

GRANDMA: *(Flips* GAGA *so she also rolls downstage)* You may have some juice.

ACT TWO

(A soft-sculpture orange juice pitcher on a long bamboo pole appears. It is just out of the CHILDREN's *reach. The* CHILDREN *stretch and reach for it.)*

GRANDMA: See the lovely cold orange juice Grandma has poured for you?

GARFIELD: We can't reach it.

GRANDMA: Why not?

GARFIELD: You're holding it up too high.

GRANDMA: Yes, I am, aren't I?

GAGA: Can we jump for it, Grandma?

GRANDMA: *(Moves as she teaches)* My grandchildren don't misbehave indoors so much as to jump. You may only jump outdoors if there is a flash flood and you have to jump over moving water to get to dry land. Jumping is unseemly.

CHILDREN: *(They run together, hug, and cower.)* Yes, Ma'am. Arggggggghhhhhh!

GRANDMA: That's not the right saying either.

GAGA: We don't know what to say. We're hot and thirsty.

GRANDMA: And Grandmother has what you want. *(Alluding to the juice)*

CHILDREN: Please?

GRANDMA: That's part of it.

CHILDREN: Please, Grandmother?

GRANDMA: You're getting warm.

CHILDREN: Please, Grandmother, may we have some juice?

GRANDMA: *(Crosses to* GAGA *and* GARFIELD, *leans down between them)* If you tell me who you were playing with.

GARFIELD: Just some kids.

GRANDMA: *(Stiffly pulls away)* Children are not kids. Kids are animals.

GAGA: Oh, please, Grandmother, may we have some juice?

GRANDMA: *(Pets* CHILDREN's *heads)* Of course my darling grandchildren may have some juice. *(Grabs their hair)* Who were they?

GAGA: They live in the house down by the woods.

GRANDMA: The Hunts? The Hunt children?

GARFIELD: Yes. We had such a good time. We went to the woods with the Hunt children and the Gibb children.

GRANDMA: You aren't supposed to go into the woods without an adult.

GAGA: *(Stands)* Jimmy Gibb is thirteen.

GRANDMA: Thirteen is not adult.

GAGA: He's real big. This big. He's bigger than you are.

GRANDMA: *(Threatens* GAGA *with wooden spoon which she has in her apron;* GAGA *ducks.)* Not bigger. He could be taller.

GAGA: He's taller and he's bigger.

GRANDMA: What did you play in the woods?

GARFIELD: It was so much fun. Give us some juice and we'll play it with you.

ACT TWO

GRANDMA: You don't play with me. *(Gestures to floor.* GAGA *knows the signal and kneels next to* GARFIELD.*)* I will teach you. I will instruct you. *(She shoves* CHILDREN *to their hands and knees.)* I will read to you *(Pulls* CHILDREN *up by the collars)* and correct you *(She slaps them down again, bellies to floor.)* so that you may be a credit to our family, but we won't play together. *(She walks away.)*

GAGA: But it's so much fun. We played a long time and we laughed, and it felt so good Grandma. You'd really like it.

GRANDMA: *(Bops* GAGA *on the head)* Grandmother!

GAGA: I'm sorry, I forgot. Grandmother! This game is so neat. It has girls and boys, big kids and little kids.

GRANDMA: *(Bops* GAGA *harder; she falls to floor.)* Children.

GARFIELD: Big children and little children and it makes you scream and jump. It's more fun than tickling or Kick the Can.

*(*GAGA *signals her brother not to say; she covers his mouth.)*

GRANDMA: What game is it?

GAGA: Can we have our juice now?

GRANDMA: What game is it?

GARFIELD: *(Frees himself from* GAGA*'s hold)* Down Below.

GRANDMA: What? *(*CHILDREN *are silent.* GRANDMA *tickles* CHILDREN.*)* What's the name of the game?

GARFIELD: They call it Down Below. But you have to go down into the hideout cave to play it.

GAGA: First you pile on lots of leaves and soft cedar tree branches, and then you take off all your clothes and we each have a flashlight, but you can only shine the light....

(The CHILDREN look at each other, giggle, and respond in unison.)

BOTH: Down Below.

(Juice on pole disappears.)

GARFIELD: Grandmother, we told you! Our juice!

GRANDMA: *(With great disgust, moves away from CHILDREN)* This is disgusting. *You* are disgusting! Do you hear me! You are disgusting. I don't know how I'm going to tell your father. He works so hard for you, he went to medical school for you. He worked every night, all night, twenty-four hours a day, seven days a week, fifty-two weeks a year for six years so that he could afford to have you and bring you up to be a credit to our family. Do you know who you are? *(Crosses to CHILDREN)* Do you? *(Bops GAGA on head)* Do you? *(Bops GARFIELD)* You are a Goon and Goons do not play Down Below with riff raff. Goons do not play Down Below until they marry. Goons do not dirty themselves with animals from bad neighborhoods. *(Moves away in disgust)* You could be diseased! Take off your clothes! Grandmother will have to scald and scour you so you will be clean again to meet your father. *(As she crosses to SINK, her activity is interrupted.)*

GARFIELD: We're hot and thirsty.

GRANDMA: *(Pulls out a wooden spoon and threatens them)* Take off your clothes you naughty disgusting children. If I scrub it all off and you promise never to play Down Below again, perhaps I will see about giving you half a glass of juice.

GAGA: *(Gets up, implores)* Oh, please? We didn't know it was bad. How could it be bad, it was so much fun?

ACT TWO 51

We laughed and rolled in the leaves and we had such a good time. We felt so good. Don't you want to feel good too?

GRANDMA: *(Hits GAGA with spoon; GAGA falls to knees.)* Take off your clothes, I said. You're probably covered with ticks!

GARFIELD: *(Shows mushrooms)* We brought you some mushrooms.

GRANDMA: *(Smacks GARFIELD's extended hands with spoon)* Poison! You want to poison me, too, as well as disappoint me? Do you have any idea how much you've hurt and disappointed your old grandmother? Do you realize what you are going to make me do? I'm heartsick. Heartsick.

(Playing on their sympathy, GRANDMA appears to become very weak; she retires to sit on teeter-totter.)

GAGA: *(Moves to her)* They're morel mushrooms, Grandmother. The Porterhouses love them. We brought enough for them and for our family. And we're going to set up a stand to sell the rest.

GRANDMA: *(With sudden strength)* Take off your clothes. You are not going into business! *(Beats GAGA to floor)* Your father is a doctor, *(Hits GARFIELD)* your grandfather was a dentist, and *(Knocks them to their hands and knees)* your great-grandfather sold cocaine to Sigmund Freud! Take off your clothes.

(SINK enters. GRANDMA pours and shakes Ajax, ammonia, and other abrasives into the SINK. She turns on the hot water and stirs. She holds up a giant steel wool pad in her hand.)

(GAGA and GARFIELD hug each other for dear life.)

GARFIELD: Arrgghh, that smells so bad.

GRANDMA: Come here and stand in this sink!

CHILDREN: It's steaming.

GRANDMA: I'll say it's steaming, and so will your butts be. You'll never ever play Down Below again. Get in the sink and start scrubbing.

CHILDREN: I'm afraid.

GRANDMA: I'm afraid too. I'm afraid you'll turn into wild uncontrollable children and the police will have to come and spank you and take you to jail for the whole town to come and see how bad you are.
(She forces CHILDREN into sink, beating them with wooden spoon.)

CHILDREN: *(In unison)* No Goon has ever been in jail!

GRANDMA: Sit in that sink! Sit in that sink! Sit in it! *(Loses control and beats them unmercifully, forcing them into the scalding water. Uses steel wool to scour backs and bottoms.)* You're such bad children you need steel wool to scour out the ticks and all the germs. You're never ever to play with those children again, you're never ever to go into the woods again. Do you hear me? Do you hear me? (CHILDREN *screaming.*) And you're never ever to tell your father or your mother what you did. And if you never *ever* tell your mother or father what disgusting things you did in the woods, your grandmother who loves you will never tell your mother or father how you have disappointed them. *(Stops scrubbing)* I will keep your secret. You want Grandmother to keep your secret. You want to behave, don't you? *(Uses steel wool again)* Don't you?

CHILDREN: *(Screaming)* Yes, yes. Oh please stop! Oh no. No!

GRANDMA: Cross your heart and hope to die, you will not tell your mother or father that you went in the woods and Grandmother had to punish you.

CHILDREN: We promise. We promise.

GRANDMA: *(Still scrubbing their boiling flesh with steel wool)* Cross your heart and hope to die.

CHILDREN: Cross my heart and hope to die.

GRANDMA: You promise you will never mention what happened today?

CHILDREN: I promise. I promise.

GRANDMA: Good. That's good. *(Lowers edge of* SINK *and pushes the weak and whimpering* CHILDREN *out onto the floor)* You want to behave, don't you? *(Pushes* SINK *back to wall)* And for being good after being so very naughty, Grandmother, who loves you, will give you each a nice big glass of juice. *(Crosses to teeter-totter and sits)* I'll have some too. I seem to be a little warm. Put on your clothes.

GARFIELD: I'm bleeding. I'm bleeding.

GRANDMA: Put on your clothes. Fresh blood is sterile.

(CHILDREN *put on clothes. They faint as they reach for juice.)*

(JUNE *enters with large soft-sculpture grocery bag — soft vegetables are visible. She startles* GRANDMA.)

JUNE: *(Notices* CHILDREN *on the floor)* What happened to the children?

GRANDMA: They're having a little nap.

JUNE: In the middle of the floor? *(Sets groceries down)*

GRANDMA: They exhausted themselves playing with the wrong children.

JUNE: For crying out loud, *(Moves to* GRANDMA, *puts arms around her; they are cheek to cheek)* Mother Goon, there are no wrong children.

GRANDMA: See for yourself. They're all bloody.

JUNE: *(Crosses to* CHILDREN, *picks one up, and looks)* Oh, my God. *(Moves to other child)* Oh no! *(*JUNE *falls asleep.)*

GRANDMA: *(Picks up telephone and dials. Before making the call she excites herself—she covers the mouthpiece of the phone and hyperventilates)* Granville? *(x)* Mother. *(x)* You know how I hate to bother you at the hospital dear, but.... *(x)* we seem to be having a little emergency here at home. *(x)* Your wife is killing the children!

(x) (A synthesizer or guitar can provide touch-tone dial sound. For the conversation, guitar slides (x) provide excellent DR GOON *responses.)*

GRANDMA: *(Hangs up phone and dances a triumphant bluesy dance as she sings:)*
I'm the mother of a winner,
Such a loving son.
When we lost our father,
Granville said, 'Mother
You'll never have to be blue.
I'll always buy you dinner.'
He gave me all this: *(Shows off diamonds and fox furs)*
Three grandchildren too,
And I'm happier than you,
Yeah, I'm happier than you,
Yeah, I'm happier than you,
Happier than you—
Happier than you—
Oh yeah!

(The three VISITING NURSES *are teetering on teeter-totter. This movement is to signify that the* VISITING NURSE *van is in motion.)*

(Lights up on MARRIOTS.*)*

MR MARRIOT: *(Holding his hand as if it's a C.B. microphone)* Come in Flying V. Is that your handle? Flying V, come in. This is Dandelion Killer calling

ACT TWO

Flying V. I think I have an emergency. Come in Flying V? Dandelion Killer calling Flying V.

(Throughout this scene the VISITING NURSES *mimic passing C.B. microphone around.* NURSE 1 *is driving.)*

NURSE 2: This is Flying V—we hear you, come in Dandelion.

MR MARRIOT: Hello V. The Humane Society said you people could do something about kids getting hurt.

NURSE 1: Ask him for specific details.

NURSE 2: Dandelion, this is Flying V. More details, please. What's hurting the kids?

MR MARRIOT: Their mother or their father! Kids are screaming all night and every night, sometimes in the daytime and even at dinnertime.

NURSE 2: Where?

MR MARRIOT: Next door.

NURSE 1: Where do you live?

MR MARRIOT: West Omaha. *(NOTE: This is one of the nicest, wealthiest areas of town.)*

NURSE 2: Have you witnessed the children being beaten?

MR MARRIOT: No, but it's keeping me up nights. The screaming. It's getting to me.

NURSE 2: Have you gone next door to see if you could help?

MR MARRIOT: I don't know how.

NURSE 3: Let's go.

(The VISITING NURSES *speed up their teetering.)*

NURSE 1: *(To other* VISITING NURSES*)* Not so fast, we need more facts.

NURSE 2: How long have you noticed these screams?

MR MARRIOT: Every day and night for two weeks.

NURSE 1: Have you called the police?

MR MARRIOT: I like to mind my own business. I didn't want to call the police, if they were playing the late show loud.

NURSE 1: What do you think is going on next door?

MR MARRIOT: At first I thought the wife was beating up on the kids because the husband was away so much. But now I think it's him because the screaming increases when he gets home.

NURSE 2: *(To the other* VISITING NURSES*)* A classic case.

NURSE 3: In West Omaha?

MR MARRIOT: Look, Flying V, can you help in any way or tell me what to do? I can't take it any more. If what I think's happening is really happening, I think someone's going to be killed.

NURSE 1: If you'll make a formal complaint, I can go out and try to make a call on them.

MR MARRIOT: That's great. That's just fine.

NURSE 1: The only problem is they might not let me in.

MR MARRIOT: But the children are being brutally hurt.

NURSE 1: Without concrete evidence we can't get the police to get a warrant to get in. Without gaining their confidence I can't get in to check the kids. Do you know if anyone besides the family comes and goes at the house? Has your wife been in the house?

MR MARRIOT: No. She talked to the husband when they were watering the lawn, but neither one of us has been in the house. Oh my God, the screams are

ACT TWO 57

starting again. Can't you come here, now? Should I call the police?

NURSE 2: Wait a minute, Dandelion.

NURSE 3: How's the gas?

NURSE 2: Running on empty.

NURSE 3: What if we have to get the kids to the hospital?

NURSE 1: Have to find gas, first.

MR MARRIOT: Come now! I'll siphon the gas from my three cars and have it waiting for you.

NURSE 1: You're on. *(Hands C.B. to* NURSE 3*)* Here, take his address. Where's the street map?

NURSE 2: *(Teetering speeds up)* Pray the gas lasts.

*(*VISITING NURSES *exit.)*

(The GOON *living room.* JUNE *takes her place, passed out on the teeter-totter. The* VISITING NURSES *attend to* JUNE. DR GOON *paces.* POLICE *enters.)*

POLICE: Did someone call for help?

NURSE 1: Come in, Officer. *(Moves to* POLICE*)*

DR GOON: No one called for help.

POLICE: I got a call on my C.B. I'm on my way home but I heard an S.O.S. at this address.

DR GOON: You got your wires crossed. I'm in charge here.

NURSE 1: Thanks for coming.

POLICE: What's the trouble, Ma'am.

NURSE 1: This man was hurting his wife and threatened to hit me.

POLICE: Is this a family fight? *(He backs away.)*

NURSE 1: It's assault, Officer.

DR GOON: *(Crosses to* JUNE, *embraces her, pushes* NURSE *out of his way)* This is my wife. I love her. Don't I honey? *(Throws the limp* JUNE *back onto teeter-totter and resumes pacing)* This woman's interfering here. *(*VISITING NURSES *attend to* JUNE.*)*

POLICE: Oh, it's a neighborhood argument?

NURSE 1: No, no. I want you to arrest this man. I have good reason to believe he'll hurt his wife further, possibly his children, and he could even be dangerous to himself.

POLICE: Has he hit you?

NURSE 1: No, his wife. She'll swear out a complaint.

POLICE: *(Pretends to look around the room. It is a feeble attempt; he trips and somersaults over teeter-totter.)* Which one's the wife?

DR GOON: *(Helps* POLICE *up; they shake hands.)* You look like a reasonable person. First one I've seen all day. You see, Officer, I'm Doctor Granville Goon. I'm a surgeon at the hospital and I came home to find my wife hysterical, my children bleeding, and these women making matters worse.

NURSE 3: And men.

DR GOON: *(To* NURSE 3*)* The men are talking. Shut up! *(Arm around shoulder of* POLICE*)* I'm used to trouble, Officer, and I've got things cleared up just fine. These women were....

NURSE 3: And men.

DR GOON: These women and boy were just leaving.

NURSE 3: Officer, we're Visiting Nurses.

POLICE: Everybody seems happy now. *(Starts to leave)*

ACT TWO 59

(DR GOON *sits on teeter-totter and puts* JUNE's *head on his lap.*)

POLICE: I've had a lot of experience with family arguments. Why don't you nurses run along and let the love birds make up? I got to get home to umpire Little League.

JUNE: *(Waking)* He's right, Granville. I do want to make up with you. I love you in spite of everything and....

DR GOON: *(Hits* JUNE*)* What do you mean by "everything?"

JUNE: I didn't mean to say that. I really didn't mean to say "everything".

DR GOON: *(Backhands her; she flies off teeter-totter.)* What did you mean to say?

POLICE: Hey, Doctor. I thought you said everything was under control.

DR GOON: Sorry, Officer, my hand slipped.

POLICE: Are you sassing me?

DR GOON: Not you. Besides, you're off duty.

POLICE: I don't like to get involved in an argument between a man and his wife but I must tell you that you've assaulted a woman in front of me.

DR GOON: She insulted me!

POLICE: That doesn't give you the right to hit her.

DR GOON: This is my house.

POLICE: I suppose it's your house and her house.

DR GOON: What I do in my house is my business.

POLICE: Assault, Doctor, is against the law.

DR GOON: *(Crosses and holds* JUNE*)* She's mine.

POLICE: She's a citizen, Doctor. She has rights.

DR GOON: She's a rotten mother. I came home to find my children hurt and bloody.

POLICE: Did *she* hurt them?

DR GOON: *(Nose to nose with* JUNE*)* That's what I'd like to know.

JUNE: *You* hurt them.

DR GOON: Not this time, I...

POLICE: Have you hurt your children in the past, Doctor?

DR GOON: I adore my children. I'm a doctor. I help people. I don't hurt them.

POLICE: *(Confidentially, to* VISITING NURSES*)* Have you suggested counseling to this couple?

NURSE 2: Yes, Officer.

POLICE: What's their attitude?

NURSE 1: Mrs Goon is willing, but Dr Goon maintains they have a happy marriage.

(POLICE *moves downstage, quite satisfied with this explanation.)*

POLICE: Why are the Visiting Nurses here?

NURSE 1: We had a report that children were being abused.

POLICE: Where are the children?

NURSE 2: We gave them first aid and put them to bed. We were just sitting down to chat with Mrs. Goon...

NURSE 3: We had to revive her. When we arrived she was out cold.

(This reinvolves the POLICE*)*

ACT TWO

POLICE: She was out cold and the children were bleeding?

DR GOON: *(Moves to* POLICE, *arm around his shoulders)* Officer, I like the way you handle yourself. *(Elbows* POLICE*)* You're trying to get to the bottom of this just as I was. You can see how confused these women are.

NURSE 3: And men.

DR GOON: *(To male nurse)* You're confused all right.

POLICE: I can understand that you were upset, Doctor.

DR GOON: *(Ushers* POLICE *to door)* Thank you, Officer. I was, and I am. But now that you've cleared things up you don't have to apologize, just go home and get on with your game. I'll clean things up. But I want you to take these nosey people with you.

POLICE: *(About to exit, he stops, turns, and takes a stand.)* Being upset doesn't call for that attitude, Doctor. Visiting Nurses don't get involved unless there's good cause.

DR GOON: This time they've made a mistake. *(Leaps onto teeter-totter)* You ladies, this is America. We have privacy laws in this country, and they were written to keep noses like yours out of a man's business. This is my family, and I can handle it. *(Jumps off)*

POLICE: *(Takes* DR GOON *by arm)* You better come downtown with me, Doctor. I think you should cool off away from home.

(DR GOON *struggles, resisting arrest. The* POLICE *lifts* DR GOON *in a restrictive hold to carry him to the station.)*

DR GOON: What do you mean by downtown?

POLICE: Down to the station. Just for twenty-four hours.

DR GOON: I'm a physician! My position!

POLICE: You should have thought of that before you hit your wife.

DR GOON: The newspapers!

POLICE: Come on, Doctor, don't compound the charges.

DR GOON: *(Freeing himself)* I demand to know the charges.

POLICE: You assaulted your wife, and now you're resisting arrest. *(In confidence, a plea)* If you come now, I'll ignore the resisting arrest charge.

DR GOON: *(An arm around the POLICE)* Can't we talk this over man-to-man?

POLICE: Do you want me to call for more officers?

DR GOON: Is your squad car out front?

POLICE: Yes.

DR GOON: Will you drive it up to the garage? I'll get my golf clubs so we'll look like friends going golfing.

POLICE: Come on, Doctor...

DR GOON: Please, please go along with me! My job! I don't want the neighbors to know. We're just getting acquainted here. Please, please? *(DR GOON frees himself and rushes to JUNE to plead with her.)*

POLICE: O.K.

DR GOON: *(Embracing JUNE)* Please tell him you won't press charges? Please, I love you. Don't let him take me to jail, please....

(JUNE falls asleep.)

DR GOON: Thanks a lot, you addict!

(DR GOON throws JUNE off teeter-totter; she does an extended number of tumbles and flips around stage.)

ACT TWO

POLICE: Let's go, Doctor. *(Throws* DR GOON *over his shoulder and carries him toward door)*

DR GOON: *(To* VISITING NURSES*)* A man's home's his castle. I'll sue you from here to Bangkok. I'll have your licenses! You can't come between a man and his family. I'll see that Bush cuts your budget!

VISITING NURSES: *(To each other)* Why do you think we ran out of gas?

*(*VISITING NURSES *make a football huddle. The huddle rotates and moves slowly left, then right.)*

NURSE 1: Is this a typical abuse case?

NURSE 2: More or less.

NURSE 3: We'll have to report first to the Child Protective Services.

NURSE 2: Those children had deep abrasions.

NURSE 1: Which one did it?

NURSE 2: The mother's so passive.

NURSE 3: Passive? She's out cold.

NURSE 1: What's she taking?

NURSE 2: A mental powder.

NURSE 1: What?

NURSE 3: I think she's tuning out with drugs, too.

NURSE 2: She's denying the reality going on here.

NURSE 3: He hit her, we *saw* it. She's denying abuse to herself *and* to her kids.

NURSE 1: But why?

NURSE 2: Stress. Usually stress related...*learned abusive behavior.*

NURSE 3: These people have big bucks. What stress could they be under?

NURSE 2: When the mother comes around, we'll try to get a history.

NURSE 1: How long will the police keep the doctor in jail?

NURSE 3: They'll be lucky if he's in the cooler over night.

(GOGO *enters with a tray and cups balanced on her head.* VISITING NURSES *notice* GOGO *and break their huddle.*)

GOGO: Hello! My daddy said I should entertain you while he was called away.

NURSE 1: Hello, did I meet you before?

GOGO: No. I was having my nap.

NURSE 1: Are your brother and sister still sleeping?

GOGO: They're getting dressed, but Grandma is dead to the world.

NURSE 2: So is your mother.

NURSE 1: *(Moves closer to better deal with* GOGO*)* Would you like to call gently to your mother, and see if you could wake her?

NURSE 2: *(Moves to other side of* GOGO*)* That might be fun. Nicer for her than if a stranger tried.

GOGO: She's often like that.

NURSE 3: How often?

GOGO: Most of each day.

NURSE 1: When does it happen?

GOGO: When the yelling starts! *(Starts screaming and biting her arm)*

ACT TWO

(VISITING NURSES make a fuss over the tea in an attempt to divert GOGO's tantrum.)

NURSE 2: That smells good.

NURSE 1: It sure does, what is it?

GOGO: Herb tea.

NURSE 3: What kind?

GOGO: Pelican *(Elbows a* NURSE*)* Punch with *(Gooses other* NURSE*)* Red Zinger.

(VISITING NURSES each take a cup. The cups are soft sculpture connected to a soft sculpture tray by Slinkies.)

NURSE 1: Sounds like a good pick-me-up.

GOGO: Mostly I drink it to get laid back.

NURSE 1: Why not? It's been a jarring day.

GOGO: Would you like honey in your tea?

(GOGO pulls soft-sculpture honey dipper from her belt and puts honey in their tea cups. VISITING NURSES each sing and sustain their thank you's. They make a chord.)

NURSE 1: Thank you.

NURSE 2: Thank you.

NURSE 3: Thank you.

(VISITING NURSES sip tea, then strangle and die a slow death from poisoning, one by one.)

GOGO: *(Throws dad a kiss)* Thanks, Dad. Your pharmacy books really work.

(GAGA and GARFIELD enter, yawning and stretching.)

GAGA: What are you doing out?

GOGO: I just served our guests, you dummies! *(Proudly alluding to bodies heaped on the floor)*

GOGO: *(Opens* JUNE's *mouth and pours down tea.* JUNE *gulps and gags.)* What's a matta, Mom, too strong? *(Laughs maniacally)* Have some honey, Mommy. *(Smears honey on her face)* Ease off into dreamland sweetie.

(JUNE *goes rigid and dies.)*

GARFIELD: *(Runs to* JUNE*)* Mommy, Mommy! *(Backs away)* She's real stiff.

GOGO: *(Stands on center of teeter-totter, acting up)* Now we have two teeter-totters.

GAGA: *(Runs to* JUNE*)* Mommy! Mommy! *(Moves away)* She's out cold.

GARFIELD: *(Notices and moves to* VISITING NURSES' *bodies)* What are these bodies on the floor?

GOGO: Bodies?

GAGA: How did they get here?

GOGO: *(Jumps off teeter-totter, hyperactively runs around stage)* Daddy left them. He's getting messy. The old boy is losing it. He used to be so neat.

GARFIELD: Where'd Daddy go?

GOGO: The police took him to jail.

GARFIELD: *(Jumping and pleading to* GOGO*)* Why? Why?

GOGO: He killed Mommy and these other bodies.

GAGA: Oh no.

(GAGA *and* GARFIELD *run to* JUNE's *body.)*

GOGO: Don't worry, he'll never get to jail. No Goon will ever be humiliated by jail. I planted an I.R.A. time bomb on the cop's motor. It should go off just as they reach Regency Circle. *(Looks at watch; she counts the seconds.)*

ACT TWO 67

(Big off-stage explosion)

GOGO: Right on time. I love plastic.

(GAGA and GARFIELD pace and worry.)

GARFIELD: What will we do? Where will we go?

GAGA: *(Turning abruptly front)* Not to Grandmother's.

GARFIELD: *(To audience)* Grandmother isn't breathing. I went into her room and jumped on her belly. Her throat rattled and her mouth burped, her bottom farted, and I ran out of the room. I thought she would hit me, but her arms were like a rag doll's.

GOGO: She loved her tea. She drank two cups with three spoonfuls of honey.

(GAGA and GARFIELD resume pacing.)

GAGA: What will we do, where will we go?

GOGO: *(On top of teeter-totter)* I'm gonna give you kids a break. Daddy gave me the keys to a beautiful van. These tootsies don't need it anymore and it fits my plan. I'm going to take you two on the vacation Daddy always promised but would never make. I'm sick of this life here, this nuclear family fake. I'm taking you to San Francisco to watch the earthquake.

GAGA & GARFIELD: *(In each other's arms)* The earthquake? Mommy!

(GAGA and GARFIELD run back to GOGO — the only other person alive. GOGO starts to maniacally pump the teeter-totter.)

GOGO: *(Chanting and jamming with 'earthquake' music as it is improvised on synthesizer)* The earthquake! Let's escalate! With Daddy and the rest of these dead, we don't need to be bored or locked into our heads. The next date on our schedule is in good old San Fran. If I time it right *(x x)* and the gas holds tight *(x x)* we'll get to the coast in time to step on the crack of the San Andreas Fault. We'll be in good position to watch the blast, as the buildings topple, and people run like rats. The fire will burn —that beautiful city will crumble. And we'll dance on the crack while the rock plates rumble.

(Lights flash to create earthquake and tidal waves. GOGO *pumps teeter-totter, sometimes in bright light, sometimes in silhouette.)*

GOGO: *(Sings)* Come on you slaves—
We're out of here before it rains.
Get down and drive, we got nothin' to lose.
Give me some brains—
I'm saving you—you high I.Q.s—
From a life of mediocrity and
Upward mobility, upward mobility blues.
We'll finance our scam
Sellin' Dad's old drugs.
We'll make all the money
Little pushers can make
And get to San Francisco
In time for the quake.

CHILDREN: We're going to San Francisco,
...And Los Angeles too.
We're rich little orphans,
We don't have a mommy,
...And we've lost our daddy, too.
And we're happier than you!
We're gonna make the earthquake!
Happier than you!
We're gonna make your guts shake!
Happier than you, happier than you,
Happier than you! GRRRRRRRR!!

("Adults" rise from the dead. Entire company performs attack/protect images, as in the opening song, while singing final chorus.)

ACT TWO

ALL: Goona goona, goona goona—
Goona goona, goona goona—
Goona goona, goona goona—
Goona goona...goona goona— *(Slowed, as if dazed. Final line to be done in macabre tableau—like zombies from the movie,* Night of the Living Dead.*)*
Goona goona...goona goona—

(Lights black out)

THE END

www.ingramcontent.com/pod-product-compliance
Lightning Source LLC
Chambersburg PA
CBHW071742040426
42446CB00012B/2436